LIT WIT

LIT WIT

Writers on Writing

Aubrey Malone

First published March 2023

ISBN 978-1-913144-45-6

:

PENNILESS PRESS PUBLICATIONS
Website:www.pennilesspress.co.uk/books

Introduction

Do we need another dictionary of literary quotations? Let's remember Reginald Hill's apothegm: 'Like underpants in the Urals, you can never have enough of them.'

Philip Larkin (wisely?) liked to say books were 'a load of crap.' So why did he write so many of them? Like Larkin, many of the quoters featured in these pages have a love-hate relationship to what they do. Maybe all writers have. Writing can be a cathartic experience but it can also be a pulverising one, at least when it's not going well. Or not going at all with Writer's Block. We don't hear of 'electrician's block' or 'plumber's block' - unless it's in the sink.

The personages featured in these pages are more often than not insecure, vengeful, jealous and embittered – in other words ideal for quotation.

Lillian Hellman might not agree. 'If I had to give young writers advice,' she once remarked, 'I'd say don't listen to writers talking about writing.' If you're not a writer, then, you'll probably be the most suitable reader for this book.

'A writer should write what he has to say,' Ernest Hemingway advised, 'not talk about it.'

But Hemingway never stopped talking about it.

That's another thing you should know about writers. They contradict themselves a lot.

A

A.A. Milne
I see no future for Milne. His plots are as thin as a filleted anchovy and his construction is reminiscent of Victorian fret-work. (Dennis Bradley)

Absorption
I was reading a book called *The History of Glue.* I couldn't put it down. (Tim Vine)

Academics
Academics teach for about ten minutes a week. Then they go off and write unreadable books about things like Chaucer's use of the semicolon. (Frank McCourt)

Adaptations
A magazine editor asked me if I would consider turning one of my plays into a short story for $500. I told him that for $500 I would gladly consider turning *War and Peace* into a music-hall sketch. (Noel Coward)

Darling, they've absolutely ruined your perfectly dull play. (Tallulah Bankhead after seeing *The Fugitive Kind*, a film based on Tennessee Williams' play *Orpheus Descending*)

Adolf Hitler

I read a book called *The Secret Life of Adolf Hitler*. It told me a lot of things I never knew, like for instance the fact that when he was having sex he liked to pee on people. That put me right off him. (Martin Mor)

Advantages

When Keats was my age he'd been dead for eleven years. This gave him a clear advantage with the critics. (Joseph O'Connor)

Advice

To become a great writer there's just one thing you need to do. Avoid piles. (T.S. Eliot)

Affluence

Marlon Brando told me I wrote plays as if I didn't know there were people starving to death. I believe he's a millionaire now. (Noel Coward)

Agatha Christie

Agatha Christie has given men more pleasure in bed than any woman in history. (Nancy Banks-Smith)

To say Agatha Christie's characters are cardboard cut-outs is an insult to cardboard. (Ruth Rendell)

Agents

If you're a writer there will come at least one morning in your life when you wake up and want to kill your agent. (Bernice Rubens)

About agents: I deal direct because I will not give 10% to any son of a bitch to do what I can do better. (Ernest Hemingway)

To get a good agent you must have sold a considerable amount of material. And in order to sell a considerable amount of material you must get a good agent. Well, you get the idea. (Steve McNeil)

Publishers may apologise to authors and to other publishers, but with agents it is enough that you let them live. (Raymond Chandler)

If God had an agent the world wouldn't be built yet. It'd only be Thursday. (Jerry Reynolds)

The relationship of an agent to a publisher is akin to that of a knife to a throat. (Marvin Josephson)

When I opened the morning paper I saw someone had shot an agent. It was probably for the wrong reasons but at least it was a step in the right direction. (Raymond Chandler)

Alfred Lord Tennyson

Anyone for Tennyson? (Matthew Sturgis)

Allen Ginsberg
Ginsberg is a beard in search of a poet. (Caesar Bottom)

Appearance
He had double chins all the way down to his stomach. (Mark Twain on Oliver Wendell Holmes)

Jacqueline Susann looks like a truck driver in drag. (Truman Capote)

W.B. Yeats looked like an umbrella left behind at a picnic. (George Moore)

Articles
I wrote an 800-word article entire for *The Observer* and got to use my entire vocabulary. Twice. (Sean Hughes)

Artists
The true artist will let his wife starve, his children go barefoot and his mother drudge for his living at 70 sooner than work at anything but his art. (George Bernard Shaw)

If you are an artist that means that you denude yourself a bit every day, so that by the time you die you're stark naked with your bowels turned inside out. (Henry Miller)

Arts Centres
An Irish Arts Centre is a whitewashed basement where you might be able to buy freshly brewed coffee and some woman might know where you could go to get an abortion. (Graham Norton)

Attribution
Everything I've ever said will, in time, be credited to Dorothy Parker. (George S. Kaufman)

Auditions
I failed my audition as Romeo through a misunderstanding of a stage direction. My copy of the script said, 'Enter Juliet from the rear.' (Lester Steiner)

Auschwitz
Nothing I wrote in the thirties saved one Jew from Auschwitz. (W.H. Auden)

Alternative Careers
If I didn't have writing, I'd be running down the street hurling grenades in people's faces. (Paul Fussell)

Ambitions
James Joyce's ambition was to forge within the smithy of his conscience the uncreated conscience of his race. And then, hopefully, have it reproduced in plastic. (Frederic O'Neill)

America

What the American public always wants is a tragedy with a happy ending. (William Dean Howells)

What other culture not could have produced someone like Hemingway and not seen the joke? (Gore Vidal)

Amnesia

I loaned my friend a book about amnesia. He forgot to bring it back. (Paul Fussell)

Andre Gide

Gide had the general look of an elderly fallen angel travelling incognito. (Peter Quennel)

Animals

No animal was harmed in the making of this book. (Simon Rose)

Autobiographies

I hear my autobiography is a terrific book. One of these days I hope to get around to reading it. (Ronald Regan)

No autobiography ever went deeper than the author's Sunday clothes. (Austin O'Malley)

I used to think I was an interesting person until I got to page 35 of my autobiography and realised I had nothing else to say. (Roseanne)

I'm writing an unauthorised autobiography. I've started warning my family and friends not to talk to me. (Steven Wright)

My autobiography was written by Ian Ross. (Howard Kendall)

Authorities
I've never regarded myself as an authority on my plays just because I wrote the damn things. (Harold Pinter)

Authors
Authors are easy to get on with – if you're fond of children. (Michael Joseph)

Autographs
A man once asked me to autograph his penis. He wasn't very well endowed. I told him I'd only be able to initial it. (Truman Capote)

Avant Garde
It's one of those avant garde plays which bring the scent of boiling cabbage across the footlights and the little man in the bowler hat turns out to be God. (P.G. Wodehouse)

B

Babies
Every baby is a failed novel. (Jack Gilbert)

Bans
Some people wouldn't read a book even if it was banned. (Will Rogers)

Bananas
I have yet to meet a writer who wouldn't rather peel a banana. (Alice Thomas Ellis)

Barbara Cartland
Barbara Cartland is an animated meringue. (Arthur Marshall)

Beds
I write from my bed. So far it's worked out nicely, especially since I've started turning myself regularly to avoid bedsores. (Marian Keyes)

Beginnings
I always start writing with a clean piece of paper and a dirty mind. (Patrick Dennis)

Ben Elton
If Ben Elton can be acclaimed on 'The South Bank Show' as a lyricist for writing tripe like 'I'm so shy, how can I get my leg over?', the late Judge Dread should have been Poet Laureate. (Garry Bushell)

Bertolt Brecht
I would rather have written *Winnie the Pooh* than the collected works of Brecht. (Tom Stoppard)

Best Sellers
The biggest selling books are cookbooks and diet books. I'm going to write one called 'How Not To Eat What You've Just Prepared.' (Andy Rooney)

'Best seller' really only means 'good seller'. There can only be one best seller. All the rest are good sellers. Each succeeding book on the list is a better seller. (George Carlin)

A best seller is a book which sold well because it was selling well. (Daniel J. Boorstin)

I asked my publishers what they'd do if all my books sold out. They said, 'We'll print another ten.' (Eric Sykes)

Bible
Even if you don't believe a word of the Bible you've still got to respect the person who typed all that. (Lotus Weinstock)

The Bible tells us to forgive our enemies. It doesn't say anything about our friends. (Peter O'Toole)

I have an aspiration that some day the Bible will be in the mythology section at the back of second-hand bookshops. (Tom Reilly)

There's a Bible on the shelf there. I keep it next to Voltaire. Poison and antidote. (Bertrand Russell)

I've been reading the Bible a lot recently. For loopholes. (W.C. Fields)

Biblethumpers
Biblethumpers are all preaches and scream. (Louis Safian)

Bibliophilia

The worst thing about being a lover of books is that it brings you into contact with those who write them. (Louis Simpson)

I love being a writer but I hate the paperwork. (Peter de Vries)

Biographers

Getting a biographer to tell the truth is a bit like asking a tart to give up the game. (Trevor Howard)

Biographies

I enjoy reading biographies because I want to know all about the people who messed up the world. (Marie Dressler)

Every great person has his disciples and it's always Judas who writes the biography. (Oscar Wilde)

When I was growing up, a biography was the life of Abraham Lincoln. Today every fifth person is a legend. (Peter Falk)

Birds

Dylan Thomas once told me that poets only know two kinds of bird by sight. One is a robin and the other a seagull. The rest they had to look up. (Lawrence Durrell)

Blood
Writing is easy. All you have to do is stare at a blank piece of paper and wait until drops of blood form on your forehead. (Gene Fowler)

Books
One book is very like another, something to read and be done with. It's not a thing that matters, like print dresses or serviettes. (H.G. Wells)

There's nothing better in life than going to bed with a book - or a dishy guy who's read one. (Jilly Cooper)

The United States will never be a civilised country until we spend more money on books than we do on chewing gum. (Elbert Hubbard)

Book Borrowing
The difference between owning a book and borrowing one is that when you own it you can spill food on it. (Susan Catherine)

Bookcases
I have loads of books but no bookcase. Nobody would lend me one. (Milton Berle)

Book Clubs
I had a perfect marriage until my wife found out the Book of the Month Club didn't hold meetings. (Bob Monkhouse)

Book Lending
Never lend books. Nobody ever returns them. The only books I have in my library are those which people have lent me. (Anatole France)

Bookmarks
I was in a speed-reading accident. I hit a bookmark. (Steven Wright)

Why pay a dollar for a bookmark? Use it as one instead. (Fred Stoller)

Book Preparation
The best time to plan a book is when you're doing the dishes. (Agatha Christie)

Book Reviews
A bad book review is less important than whether it is raining in Patagonia. (Iris Murdoch)

If you get six out of six good reviews you can ask the President of the United States to sell you the White House. (Brendan Behan)

Bookshops
I once went into a bookshop and asked if they stocked *The Confessions of St. Augustine.* The assistant said, 'Who is it by?'(Hugh Leonard)

Murphy went into a bookshop and asked the salesgirl if she had a book called *How to Get On*

With Your Wife. She said, 'The Fiction section is upstairs.' (Hal Roach)

Go into any bookshop in Wales and you will be in England. (Rhys Davies)

Booker Prize
Christopher Booker is the man who invented the Booker Prize. It's his money which keeps the whole rotten show on the road, ensuring that the English novel, once the pride of our culture, remains in a permanent state of thraldom to a small group of London voluptuaries, literary lesbians and poodle-fakers. (Auberon Waugh)

My father always had doubts about the reliability of the Booker Prize until they announced that he'd won it. (Martin Amis on Kingsley)

Braille
Never offer a blind person a Matzo biscuit. They might think it's a page of Braille and start reading it. (Victor Lewis-Smith)

Builders
My favourite Irish joke concerns the worker on the building site who's asked if he knows the difference between a joist and a girder. 'Of course I do,' he says, 'Joist is the man who wrote *Ulysses*. Girder wrote *Faust*. (Mary Kenny)

C

California
You can't write comedy in California. It's not depressing enough. (Sy Benson)

Californians
The only thing Californians read is the licence plate in front of them. (Neil Simon)

Camaraderie
If you only have to deal with writers through the mail it's not so bad. It's the personal visits that are so repelling. Since you write, since they write, bingo, they expect something like a brotherhood or a sisterhood. I prefer cats as companions. (Charles Bukowski)

Canada
Canada is a great country to write poetry in because it's brutal and indifferent. Everyone is unhappy and if they're not unhappy they're dull. It gives everything a wonderful edge. (Leonard Cohen)

Career Change
I left the *Irish Press* to go into journalism. (Kevin Marron)

Carl Sandberg
Sandberg's verse reminds us of blobs of plankton brought up by deep sea dredging. (George Whicker)

Cats
I see my brother has produced a memoir. The cat in Number 70 will be writing next. (Brendan Behan)

I like heavy books for one basic reason. They can be thrown at cats. (Mark Twain)

Chapters
Autobiographies ought to begin with Chapter Two. (Ellery Sedgwick)

Charity Shops
Charity shops are where airport novels go to die. (Guy Browning)

Charles Algernon Swinburne
Swinburne stands up to his neck in a cesspool and then adds to its contents. (Thomas Carlyle)

Cheques
The best thing I ever wrote was a cheque for £5000 that didn't bounce. (Patrick Kavanagh)

Chick Lit
Chick Lit is just Mills & Boon with Wonderbras.
(Kathy Lette)

A man will give up on a book as rubbish if a
character doesn't get killed, have sex with a
stranger or show signs of having a Nazi past
within the first twenty pages. Women, on the
other hand, will stick with the chick-lit tale of
Angie, a twentysomething career girl who loves
Chardonnay and saucy flings with divine
stockbrokers but longs to marry an older doctor.
If Angle dies with a swastika on her knickers,
you could also nail the male market. (Pat
Fitzpatrick)

Children
With the birth of each child you lose two novels.
(Candida McWilliam)

Oh for an hour of Herod. (Anthony Hope after
watching a stage version of 'Peter Pan')

Choices
Why would a person take a year to write a novel
when he could just as easily buy one for a few
dollars? (Fred Allen)

Clifford Odets
Odets, where is thy sting? (George S. Kaufman)

Cocaine

I used to take so much cocaine while I was writing, it got to the point where I had to do a line to write a line. (Richard Price)

Columnists

Being a newspaper columnist is like being married to a nymphomaniac. It's great for the first two weeks. (Lewis Grizzard)

Collaboration

Shakespeare had a sad life. After all, he didn't live long enough to collaborate with Andrew Lloyd Webber. (Victoria Wood)

I wrote this book called *How to Get Along With Everybody*. Not by myself but with this other asshole jerk. (Steve Martin)

Commissions

I've been commissioned by Michael Joseph to write my autobiography. Can anyone tell me where I was between 1960 and 1974? (Jeffrey Barnard)

Commitment

The only demand I make of my reader is that he should devote his whole life to reading my works. (James Joyce)

Comparisons
Meredith is a prose Browning - and so is Browning. (Oscar Wilde)

Reading a novel by Thomas Wolfe is like making love to a 300-pound woman: if she goes on top, you're asphyxiated. (Norman Mailer)

Writing is like jumping from a plane. The worrying thing is that you don't know if you're going to come out with a parachute or a grand piano. (Joseph O'Connor)

Compensations
I've earned $47 in twenty years of writing. I think that entitles one to the privilege of a special insanity. (Charles Bukowski in 1959)

Completion
Finishing a book is like taking your child out to the yard and shooting it. (Truman Capote)

A poem is never finished, only abandoned. (Paul Valery)

Computers
Reading computer manuals without the hardware is as frustrating as reading sex manuals without the software. (Arthur C. Clarke)

Confessions
A confessional passage has probably never been written that didn't stink a little bit of the writer's pride in having given up his pride. (J.D. Salinger)

I've done a lot of horrible things in my life but I never taught creative writing. (Richard Price)

Countries
In France all writers are important. In America only the successful one is. In England no writer is important. In Australia you have to explain what a writer is. (Geoffrey Cotterell)

Couples
They were a couple you wouldn't invite home to your mother, even if you were certain that she was out. (Con Houlihan on Dylan and Caitlin Thomas)

Covers
The covers of this book are too far apart. (Ambrose Bierce)

I have a loathing for any book that doesn't have a swastika and a girl in a bikini on the cover. (Jeremy Clarkson)

Criticism
A great deal of literary criticism reads to me like a man saying 'Of course I do not like green cheese. I am very fond of brown sherry'. (G.K. Chesterton)

Critics
Unless the bastards have the courage to give you unqualified praise, I say ignore them. (John Steinbeck)

Where were you fellows when the page was blank? (Fred Allen)

The biggest critics of my books are people who never read them. (Jackie Collins)

For critics I care the five hundred thousandth part of a half-farthing. (Charles Lamb)

Critics die too soon to be force-fed into vomiting into their words. (John Osborne)

I love every bone in their heads. (Eugene O'Neill)

Curiosity
Only when one has lost all curiosity about the future has one reached the age to write an autobiography. (Evelyn Waugh)

Cyril Connolly
You don't have to be alive to write like Connolly.
(Raymond Chandler)

D

Daffodils

Depression is to me what daffodils were to Wordsworth. (Philip Larkin)

Wordsworth keeps one eye on a daffodil and the other on a canal share. (Walter Landor)

Dante

A hyena that wrote poetry in tombs. (Friedrich Nietzsche)

Dating

I'm dating again so I've been reading up on the differences between men and women. I read the Mars and Venus books and *Dating For Dummies*. That's the real difference: Women buy books. (Daryl Hogue)

Daughters

I have three daughters. As a result I played King Lear almost without rehearsal. (Peter Ustinov)

David Mamet

Any actor who tries to memorise a David Mamet play eventually wants to commit suicide. (William Macy)

Debuts
Alexander Woolcott always praised stage debuts.
He hated stoning the first cast. (Walter Winchell)

Dedications
I dedicate this book to my daughter Leonora,
without whose never-failing sympathy and
encouragement it would have been finished in
half the time. (P.G. Wodehouse)

Delusions
I'm the kind of writer people think other people
are reading. (V.S. Naipaul)

H.L. Mencken suffers from the delusion that he's
H.L. Mencken. There is no cure for a disease of
that magnitude. (Maxwell Bodenheim)

Depression
His attitude to most accredited sources of
pleasure would make Scrooge seem frolicsome.
(John Carey on Philip Larkin)

Desires
What every writer really wants is to have letters
printed in the papers. When he realises he can't
achieve this he drops down a rung of the ladder
and writes novels. (P.G. Wodehouse)

I always wanted to write a book that ended with
the word 'mayonnaise.' (Richard Brautigan)

D.H. Lawrence
Lawrence was a cock-freak who never had nerve enough to face the world. Instead he looked at it through a soul-soothing whirl of sex proteins. (Charles Bukowski)

Diaries
Diaries are full of indispensable information, such as the recommended tyre pressure for North Korea. (Leslie Mallory)

To write a diary every day is like returning to one's own vomit. (Enoch Powell)

Dictionaries
A new dictionary for masochists has just come out. It lists all the words, but not in alphabetical order. (Frank Tyger)

The other night I was reading the dictionary. I thought it was a poem about everything. (Steven Wright)

I bought a dictionary because I'm lousy at spelling. Now I don't know where to find the words I'm looking for. (Thomas Farrell)

Didacticism
Didactic writers sell their birthright for a pot of message. (Kenneth Tynan)

Difficulty
Writing is the hardest way to earn a living with the possible exception of wrestling alligators. (Olin Miller)

Disappointment
I bought a book called *Dealing with Disappointment*. It was filled with empty pages. (Milton Berle)

DIY
I was doing some DIY in the house and ran into a problem with a shelf. I went to the library and said, 'Have you any books on shelves?' The librarian said, 'They all are.' (Ivor Dembina)

Dogs
My dog ate *Of Mice and Men* but was unable to finish *Moby Dick*. (George Steinbeck)

I asked a woman why she had two Seeing Eye dogs. She said one was for reading. (Jonathan Katz)

Outside a dog a book is a man's best friend. Inside a dog it's too dark to read. (Groucho Marx)

My dog had very little Latin but had, as a pup, devoured Shakespeare - in a tasty leather binding. (Henny Youngman)

To call Richard Brautigan's poetry doggerel is an insult to dogs. (Lazlo Coakley)

Dove Cottage
No visit to Dove Cottage is complete without examining the house where Hazlitt's father, a Unitarian minister of strong liberal views, attempted to put his hand up Dorothy Wordsworth's skirt. (Alan Coren)

Drama Critics
I don't think anyone can take a drama critic's job seriously. It is by definition a nonsense. He is simply a member of the audience who gets free tickets. (Bernard Muller)

If Attila the Hun were alive today he'd be a drama critic. (Edward Albee)

Like all good drama critics, we retired to the pub across the road. (Eric Cross)

Drinking
The main character in Kafka's *Metamorphosis* wakes up one morning in Prague to discover he's a slug. This will be a sensation familiar to anyone who's drunk Budvar for 50 cents a pint in the Czech capital. (Pat Fitzpatrick)

Alcohol is like love. The first kiss is magic, the second is intimate. After that you just take the girl's clothes off. (Raymond Chandler)

Some American writers who've known each other for years have never met in the daytime or when both were sober. (James Thurber)

The last person I want to drink with is a writer. I've found more gut life in old newsboys, janitors or the kid waiting window at an all-night taco stand. (Charles Bukowski)

Drollness
Very nice, but there are dull stretches. (Comte de Rivaro on a two-line poem)

Dyslexia
When I was young I used to write about my dyslexia in a dairy. (Andrea Ferris)

E

Eagerness
There's a great deal of difference between the eager man who wants to read a book and the tired man who wants a book to read. (G.K. Chesterton)

Edith Sitwell
Three-quarters of her poetry is gibberish. I mustn't say this, however, or the dove of peace will shit on me. (Noel Coward)

Editing
You could compile the worst book in the world entirely out of selected passages from the best writers in the world. (G.K. Chesterton)

Editorials
Who writes the *Irish Times* editorials? They read like they've been done by an old woman sitting in a bath with the water getting cold around her fanny. (Charles Haughey)

Editors
Trust your editor and you'll sleep on straw. (John Cheever)

If they have a popular thought they have to go into a darkened room and lie down until it passes.

(Kelvin Mackenzie on editors of upmarket newspapers)

Edmund Wilson
Reading Wilson's criticism is like reading second-rate gospels written by someone who's out on parole. (Ernest Hemingway)

Ego
Balzac was so conceited he raised his hat every time he spoke about himself. (Robert Broughton)

Never have I encountered so much pretension with so little to show for it. (W.B. Yeats after meeting James Joyce)

He was his own greatest invention and he worshipped his Maker. (John Lahr on Kenneth Tynan)

Electric Typewriters
The first time I tried an electric typewriter I felt as if I'd been put at the controls of a Concorde after five minutes tuition. (Philip Larkin)

Embarrassment
A man once bought a packet of condoms in a shop because he was too embarrassed to buy my autobiography. (Terry Wogan)

Encyclopaedias

When I was in college I sold encyclopaedias. The librarian was really pissed off when she found out. (Brian Kiley)

I'm not going to buy my kids an encyclopaedia. Let them walk to school like I did. (Yogi Berra)

Endings

I write the endings of my books first. Nobody reads one to get to the middle. (Mickey Spillane)

I always read the last page of a book first so that if I die before I finish it I'll know how it turned out. (Nora Ephron)

Enemies

If you're seriously bent on becoming a Dublin writer it's important to make an enemy as soon as you can or nobody will take you seriously. (David Kenny)

He hasn't an enemy in the world but none of his friends like him. (Oscar Wilde on George Bernard Shaw)

English Novels

An English novel is a story in which two people fall in love and then complain to each other about it for 400 pages. (Colin Bowles)

Envelopes
A good many writers make the mistake of enclosing a stamped addressed envelope with their submissions that's large enough for their manuscripts to come back in. This is far too much of a temptation for an editor. (Ring Lardner)

Epigrams
An epigram is only a wisecrack that's played at Carnegie Hall. (Oscar Levant)

Erasers
Jack Kerouac was a high school athlete who went from Lowell, Massachusetts to Skid Row, losing his eraser en route. (John Ciardi)

Ernest Hemingway
I read Hemingway for the first time in the early forties. Something about bells, balls and bulls. (Vladimir. Nabokov)

Hemingway was always willing to lend a helping hand to the person above him on the ladder. (F. Scott Fitzgerald)

I see Hemingway as a fellow who practised ballet behind closed doors. (Charles Bukowski)

Errata
This erratum slip has been inserted by mistake. (Oliver Herford)

Ethics
Like everyone who talks of ethics all day long, one could not trust Arthur Koestler half an hour with one's wife, one's best friend, one's manuscript or one's wine merchant. (Cyril Connolly)

I asked the librarian if she had any books on ethics. She said they'd all been nicked. (Julian Corlett)

Evelyn Waugh
Evelyn Waugh looked like a letter delivered to the wrong address. (Malcolm Muggeridge)

Waugh had all the jauntiness of an orchestra fiddling away for dear life on a sinking ship. (Edmund Wilson)

Evolution
How stupid of me not to have thought of that! (Thomas Huxley after reading Darwin's *Origin of Species*)

Excess
The poet William Blake said 'The road to excess leads to the palace of wisdom'. If that's true, I must be the most intelligent guy on the planet. (Kris Kristofferson)

Explanations
Dylan hated people intellectualising his work. One time someone asked him to explain his poem 'Ballad of the Long-Legged Bait.' He replied, 'It's a description of a gigantic fuck.' (Caitlin Thomas on her husband)

Expletives
One of the most pleasing experiences of my literary life was writing 'Yeats' and 'fuck' in the same sentence. (Joseph O'Connor)

F

Faces
After a certain number of years our faces become our biographies. (Cynthia Ozick)

Fakery
There's a hell of a lot of fakery in this poetry business. 'I'll print you if you print me. And wouldn't you like to read before a select group of homosexuals?' (Charles Bukowski)

Fame
The best fame is a writer's one. It's enough to get a table at a good restaurant but not enough that you get photographed while you're eating. (Fran Lebowitz)

It took me fifteen years to discover I had no talent for writing but I couldn't give it up because by that time I was too famous. (Robert Benchley)

Family Trees
If I were to write to Emile Zola it would be to advise him, now that the family tree of the Rougon-Macquarts is complete, to go and hang himself from the highest branch. (Alphonse Daudet)

Fatigue
A man told me he'd been reading my works all his life. I observed that he must be very tired. (Samuel Beckett)

Favourites
My favourite book was *Everything You Always Wanted to Know About Sex But Were Afraid to Ask*. I was not afraid to ask. (Drew Barrymore)

My favourite poem is the one that starts with the words, 'Thirty Days Hath September.' Unlike most poems, it actually tells you something. (Groucho Marx)

My favourite book is my pension one. (Jimmy Savile)

Fear
I've always been afraid I was going to tap the world on the shoulder for twenty years and when it finally turned around, I was going to forget what I had to say. (Tom Waits)

Feeling
All bad poetry springs from genuine feeling. (Oscar Wilde)

Fiction
The difference between reality and fiction is that fiction has to make sense. (Tom Clancy)

Films

One of the great things about books is sometimes there are some fantastic pictures made of them. (George Bush)

Some of today's films are so long it takes less time to read the book. (Leopold Fechtner)

Finnegans Wake

Joyce talked to himself in his sleep. Hence, *Finnegans Wake*. (Oliver St. John Gogarty)

My wife thought it sounded like someone drunk in a Manchester snug. (Anthony Burgess)

Only a new cure for the clap can possibly justify all the circumambient peripherisation. (Ezra Pound)

It's just one long spelling mistake. (Ernest Cox)

First Editions

There's nothing as rare as a Woollcott first edition. Except perhaps a Woollcott second edition. (Franklin Adams)

First Novels

Today publishers are reluctant to publish first novels by anyone who has not been, at the very least, a movie star or serial killer. (Gore Vidal)

Fish
No self-respecting fish would ever be caught wrapped inside a Murdoch newspaper. (Mike Royko)

Great Moments in literature: In 1936 Ernest Hemingway, while trout fishing, caught a carp and decided not to write about it. (Roger Guindon)

Flies
Books of poems lying around are handy for killing persistent irritating flies. (Geoffrey Grigson)

Footnotes
Footnotes in a book are like banknotes in the stockings of a harlot. (Walter Benjamin)

A footnote is like running downstairs on your wedding night to answer the doorbell. (H.L. Mencken)

I haven't read Karl Marx. I got stuck on a footnote on Page Two. (Harold Wilson)

Fortuitousness
If it hadn't been for Hitler, Bertolt Brecht would still be behind the bacon counter at Oberammergau. (Frank Muir)

Francis Bacon
If Bacon wrote Shakespeare, who wrote Bacon? (Nigel Rees)

Frankfurt Book Fair
An author at the Frankfurt Book Fair is basically an inconvenience. (Joe O'Connor)

Franz Kafka
The trouble with Kafka is that he didn't know the word 'Kafkaesque.' (Alan Bennett)

Freelancers
The advantage of being a freelance writer is that you're free to starve anywhere you like. (S.J. Perelman)

The freelance writer is someone who's paid per piece, per word, or perhaps. (Robert Benchley)

Free Verse
Writing free verse is like playing tennis with the net down. (Robert Frost)

I recently bought a book of free verse. For twelve dollars. (George Carlin)

French Intellectuals
Albert Camus was a philosopher, novelist and playwright. Like many French intellectuals, he

kept goal for Algeria and died in a car crash.
(William Donaldson)

G

Gabriel Faure
Faure writes the sort of music a pederast might hum while raping a choirboy. (Marcel Proust)

Galilie Galileo
If Galileo had said in verse that the world moved, the Inquisition might have left him alone. (Thomas Hardy)

Gas Chambers
Sometimes I think authors should write one book and then be put in a gas chamber. (John Marquand)

Gas Meters
This fellow called at my door and said, 'I'd like to read your gas meter.' I said, 'Whatever happened to the classics?' (Emo Phillips)

Genius
I was a genius and therefore unemployable. (Patrick Kavanagh)

It takes a lot of time to be a genius. You have to sit around so much doing nothing. (Gertrude Stein)

Any fool can write poetry but it takes a genius to get it published. (Horace Jones)

George Bernard Shaw

Shaw is the most poisonous of all the poisonous haters in England; a despiser and distorter of the plain truths whereby men live; a topsy-turvy perverter of all human relationships; a menace to ordered social thought and ordered social life; an irresponsible braggart; a blaring self-trumpeter; the idol of opaque intellectuals and thwarted females; a calculus of contrariwise; flibberty gibbet Pope of chaos; portent and epitome of this generation's moral and spiritual disorder. (Henry Arthur Jones)

Shaw writes like a Pakistani who learned English when he was twelve years old in order to become a chartered accountant. (John Osborne)

His brain is a half-inch layer of champagne poured over a bucket of Methodist near-beer. (Benjamin de Casseres)

The way Shaw believes in himself is very refreshing in these atheistic days when so many people believe in no God at all. (Israel Zangwill)

George Meredith

As a writer he's mastered everything except language. (Oscar Wilde)

George Moore

Moore leads his readers to the latrine and locks them in. (Oscar Wilde)

George Orwell
Orwell couldn't blow his nose without moralising on conditions in the handkerchief industry. (Cyril Connolly)

George Sand
Sand's ideas on morals have the same delicacy of feeling as those of janitresses and kept women. (Charles Baudelaire)

Ghost Writing
I see Naomi Campbell has ghost-written a book. If only I could get someone to ghost-read it for me. (Mark Lamarr)

Gifts
The most essential gift for a writer is a good inbuilt, shock-proof shit detector. (Ernest Hemingway)

Golf
If only I'd taken up golf earlier and devoted my life to it. Instead of writing books I might have got my handicap down to 18. (P.G. Wodehouse)

Graham Greene
He was going pretty good there for a while but now he's just a whore with a crucifix over his bed. (Ernest Hemingway on Greene's later work)

Grammar
George Moore wrote brilliant English until he discovered grammar. (Oscar Wilde)

Never correct a man's grammar in bed. (Dodie Meeks)

Grand Canyon
I remember coming across George Bernard Shaw at the Grand Canyon and finding him refusing to admire it. He was jealous. (J.B. Priestley)

Greatness
Are there any writers on the literary scene whom I consider truly great? Yes. Truman Capote. (Truman Capote)

Growing Up
He went from youth to senility without going through manhood. (Ernest Hemingway on Scott Fitzgerald)

H

Hair

I was going to buy a book on hair loss but the pages kept falling out. (Jay London)

Hamlet

Hamlet is the product of a drunken savage's imagination. (Voltaire)

The central problem in *Hamlet* is whether the critics are mad or only pretending to be. (Oscar Wilde)

Hamlet is the tragedy of tackling a family problem too soon after college. (Tom Masson)

My intention is to do to Hamlet what Hamlet longed to do to his mother. (Play director Arthur Smith)

I turned *Hamlet* down. It was going to take up too much of my drinking time. (Richard Harris)

Hardbacks

The shelf life of the modern hardback writer is somewhere between the milk and the yoghurt. (Calvin Trillin)

Harold Robbins
Harold Robbins is able to turn an unplotted unworkable manuscript into an unplotted unworkable manuscript with lots of sex. (Tom Volpe)

Hearts
One must have a heart of stone to read the death of Little Nell without laughing. (Oscar Wilde on Dickens' *Little Dorrit*)

Height
I bought a book once called *How to Be Taller*. All the pages were blank except for the one that said 'Stand on the book.' (Petra Handey)

Henry James
James writes fiction as if it were a painful duty. (Oscar Wilde)

James was one of the nicest old ladies I ever met. (William Faulkner)

A vast panorama of tintinnabulations, a molten sheen of iridescent acerbities, a mumbo-jumbo of tortured hieroglyphics, a frazzled counterpane of dyspeptic arabesques. (Henry Miller)

H.G. Wells

Wells throws information at the reader as if emptying a chamber pot from a window. (Henry James)

I stopped thinking about H.G. Wells when he became a thinker. (Lytton Strachey)

Heinrich Heine

Heine so loosened the corsets of the German language that today every little salesman can fondle her breasts. (Karl Kraus)

Hollywood

Being a writer in Hollywood gives one the opportunity to fly first class, be treated like a celebrity, sit around the pool and be betrayed. (Ian McEwan)

Homosexuals

People like it when I write about dead queers but not when I write about live ones. (Thom Gunn)

The Bible contains six admonishments to homosexuals and 362 to heterosexuals. This doesn't mean God doesn't love heterosexuals. It just means they need more supervision. (Lynn Larner)

After Oxford, Philip Larkin's homosexual feelings evaporated and were henceforth diverted into his odd choice of socks. (Alan Bennett)

Horatio Alger
Alger wrote the same novel 135 times. (George Juergens)

Houses
It was the sort of house where they had six Bibles and no corkscrew. (Mark Twain)

How-To Books
Books are useless. I've only read one. It was called *To Kill a Mockingbird* and it gave me absolutely no insight into how to do that. (Homer Simpson)

Humility
I once wrote a book on humility. I think it's my best. (Michael Crawley)

Humour
Susan Sontag's sense of humour is about as well developed as that of King Kong. (William F. Buckley)

Bernard Levin writes perfect English but he's about as funny as John the Baptist going shopping for balaclavas. (Jaci Stephen)

The humour of Dostoevsky is the humour of a bar-loafer who ties a kettle to a dog's tail. (W. Somerset Maugham)

Hyphens

If you take hyphens seriously you will surely go mad. (John Benbow)

I

Ideas
Neil Simon didn't have an idea for a play this year but he wrote it anyway. (Walter Kerr in 1967)

Ignorance
I don't know how to write a poem. If I did, I wouldn't be able to write one. (Dannie Abse)

Illegibility
Horace Greeley wrote so illegibly that a fired employee used his letter of discharge as a reference for another job. (Robert Hendrickson)

Importance
In America it's considered a lot more important to be a great Batman than a great Hamlet. (Kevin Kline)

There are three books my daughter felt were the most important influences in her life: the Bible, her mother's cookbook, and her father's chequebook. (Joyce Mattingley)

If you have something of importance to say, for God's sake start at the end. (Sarah Duncan)

Infinitives

Remember to never split an infinitive. (William Safire)

I don't split infinitives. When I get to work on them I break them into little pieces. (Jimmy Durante)

Influences

Gore Vidal - that brilliant American author whose name is sometimes mentioned in the same breath as Shakespeare, Proust, Gide, Liberace... and Larry Grayson. (Auberon Waugh)

We have met too late. You're too old to be influenced by me. (James Joyce to W.B. Yeats after their one and only encounter)

If it were thought that anything I wrote was influenced by Robert Frost, I would take that particular work, shred it and flush it down the toilet, hoping not to clog the pipes. (James Dickey)

Insanity

It is said that Hamlet is the first modern man, so obviously he must be insane. (Terry Hands)

Insomnia

When I can't sleep I read a book by Steve Allen. (Oscar Levant)

Inspiration.
The best training for a young writer is to go out and hang himself. He should then cut himself down. At least he'll have the story of the hanging to commence with. (Ernest Hemingway)

Writing is no trouble. You just jot down ideas as they occur to you. The jotting is simplicity itself. It's the occurring that's difficult. (Stephen Leacock)

Insults
Thou eunuch of language, thou pimp of gender, thou pickle herring in the puppet show of nonsense. (Robert Burns to a critic of one of his poems)

You're not a writer. You couldn't write 'fuck' on a dusty Venetian blind. (Coral Browne to an acquaintance)

Integrity
I'm the only 'principal' he ever had. (Jeffrey Archer's old headmaster at Braserose College, Sir Nos Hall)

Intelligence
Great novels are always a little more intelligent than their authors. (Milan Kundera)

Aldous Huxley was a stupid person' s idea of a clever person. (Elizabeth Bowen)

Invitations
Mr T., you are a cunt. Come and have dinner with me. (Noel Coward to Kenneth Tynan in 1959)

Ireland
In Ireland a writer is a looked upon as a failed conversationalist. (George Moore)

Irish People
The Irish bottle up their grievances rather than deal with them. When they have enough saved up, they either go mad or write a book. (Frank McNally)

Asking an Irishman to write a book about Ireland is like telling a cannibal chief that he must cook his granny for special guests. (Alan Bestic)

Irish Literary Movements
An Irish literary movement is half a dozen writers who cordially detest one another. (George Moore)

Irony
I didn't write the song 'I Write the Songs'. (Barry Manilow)

IQ

I've written a book called *How To Raise Your IQ By Eating Gifted Children*. (Lewis Frumkes)

Many very fine writers are intimidated when they have to write the way people really talk. Actually it's quite easy. Simply lower your IQ by fifty and start typing. (Steve Martin)

J

Jam
A careful reading of *Anna Karenina,* if it achieves nothing else, will teach you how to make very tasty strawberry jam. (Julian Mitchell)

James M. Cain
Everything James Cain touches smells like a billygoat. He's the kind of writer I detest, a *faux naif*, a Proust in greasy overalls, a dirty little boy with a piece of chalk in the front parlour and buckets of slop at the back door. (Raymond Chandler)

James Joyce
Joyce was an essentially private man who wished his indifference to public notice to be universally recognised. (Tom Stoppard)

The reason James Joyce is inaudible is because he spends most of his time talking to himself. (G.K. Chesterton)

Joyce is a living argument in defence of my contention that it was a mistake to establish a separate university for the aborigines of Ireland, for the corner boys who spit into the Liffey. (John Pentland Mahaffy)

Mr Joyce tries to put everything in. I try to leave everything out. (Samuel Beckett)

Jane Austen

Austen's books are absent from my library. That omission alone would make a fairly good library out of a library that hadn't a book in it. (Mark Twain)

I am the only person to have been blown off a lavatory during the blitz while reading Jane Austen. (Kingsley Martin)

It seems a great pity they allowed Jane Austen die a natural death. (Mark Twain)

J.D. Salinger

The greatest mind ever to stay in prep school. (Norman Mailer)

Jeffrey Archer

Whenever I want a good read I get one of Jeffrey Archer's novels and stand on it so I can reach the good books. (Steven Norris)

Archer is proof of the proposition that in each of us there lurks a bad novel. (Julia Critchley)

Is there no beginning to your talents? (Clive Anderson to Archer in 1991)

The last time I was in Spain I got through six Archer novels. I must remember to take enough toilet paper next time. (Bob Monkhouse)

Archer tells us he wrote his last book on a Tuesday. What I want to know is, what *time* on Tuesday. (Hugh Leonard)

Job
I read the Book of Job last night. I don't think God comes well out of it. (Virginia Woolf)

Jobs
My ideal job would be landlord in a bordello. The company is good and the mornings are quiet, which is the best time to write. (William Faulkner)

Joe Orton
The Grandma Moses of the rubbish dump. (*The Sunday Telegraph*)

John Dos Passos
Dos Passos is like a man who's trying to run in a dozen directions at once, succeeding thereby merely in standing still and making a noise. (V.S. Pritchett)

Jokes
I was once gratified to receive a cheque from a magazine for a joke I'd stolen from one of its own pages. (Bernard Braden)

Jonathan Swift

Jonathan Swift was something of a rarity among famous Irish writers in that he actually lived and wrote in Ireland (Evan McHugh)

Joseph Conrad

He spent his time looking for the *mot juste* – and then killing it off. (Ford Madox Ford)

One of the surest signs of his genius is that women detest his books (George Orwell)

Reading Joseph Conrad is like gargling with broken glass. (Hugh Leonard)

Journalism

Journalism is a cheap catch-all for fuckoffs and misfits, a false doorway to the backside of life, a filthy, piss-ridden little hole nailed off by the building inspectors, but just deep enough for a wino to curl up from the sidewalk and masturbate like a chimp in a zoo-cage. (Henry Miller)

Journalists

Journalists write because they have nothing to say, and have something to say because they write. (Karl Kraus)

The essence of a journalist: no ideas and the ability to express them perfectly. (Karl Kraus)

Where journalists are concerned, there's no word so derogatively stinking that it sums up the congested stink of their constipation. (Caitlin Thomas)

Journalists have faces that look like road maps of downtown Warsaw. (Guy Browning)

Every journalist has a great novel within him - and an excellent reason why it never got out. (John Timpson)

Journalists lie in the sun all day. Then they go home to their typewriters and lie some more. (Frank Sinatra)

If a person isn't talented enough to become a novelist, smart enough to be a lawyer and his hands shake too much to perform operations, he becomes a journalist. (Norman Mailer)

Joyce Carol Oates
Oates is a joke monster who ought to be beheaded in a public auditorium. She does all the graffiti in the men's room in every public toilet from here to California and back, stopping in Seattle on her way. (Truman Capote)

J.R. Tolkien
His appeal is to readers with a lifelong appetite for juvenile trash. (Edmund Wilson)

Jude the Obscure
The village aesthetics brooding over the village idiot. (C.K. Chesterton)

Judith Krantz
Krantz' novels remind me of conversations between not very bright drunks. (Clive James)

K

Killers
I do a lot of reading about serial killers. Mostly 'How to' books. (Roseanne)

Kingsley Amis
There's no known cure for Kingsley Amis. (Robert Graves)

L

Language

I had a language teacher who said it's man's ability to use language that makes him the dominant species on the planet. That may be, but there's one other thing that separates us from animals. We aren't afraid of vacuum cleaners. (Jeff Stilson)

Laughter

From the moment I picked up your book until I put it down I was convulsed with laughter. Some day I intend reading it. (Groucho Marx)

Lawyers

People often ask me why I write mostly about crooked lawyers. I tell them if I wrote about honest ones I wouldn't be able to *give* my books away. (John Grisham)

Legacies

He's a writer for the ages. The ages of four to eight. (Dorothy Parker)

Lennox Robinson

Lennox Robinson was often the worse for sherry. He once queued patiently for two hours for the Bing Crosby film *Going My Way* at the Capitol

Cinema in Dublin while under the impression he was waiting for the Dalkey tram. (Hugh Leonard)

Letters
Never answer an anonymous letter. (Yogi Berra)

I have made this letter longer than usual only because I have not had the time to make it shorter. (Blaise Pascal)

Lord Chesterfield's letters teach the morals of a whore and the manners of a dancing master. (James Boswell)

My sex life is now reduced to fan letters from an elderly lesbian who wants to borrow $800. (Groucho Marx)

Libel
An author never knows when he may be served, in all innocence, with a writ for libel. 'Responsible people' testify that Lambert Simnel is really Simnel Lambert, the noted brain surgeon, or that Goshnorov of Planet X7 is a damaging portrait of Noshgorov, the admitted Soviet defector. (Anthony Burgess)

Libel letters are the Oscars of journalism. (Roisin Ingle)

Librarians
Did you hear about the librarian whose baby was overdue? She got a hefty fine. (Les Dawson)

Libraries

There are seventy million books in American libraries but the one you want is always out. (Tom Masson)

In a disastrous fire in Donald Trump's library, both books were destroyed. Sadly, one of them wasn't even coloured in. (Patricia Hyde)

In my day a juvenile delinquent was a kid who owed tuppence on an overdue library book. Now he has to practically kill someone. (Max Bygraves)

Walking in a library door is like being raped by an army. (Eileen Ni Chuilleanain)

I was at a convenience store reading a magazine when the clerk came up to me and said, 'This isn't a library'. I said, 'Okay, I'll speak louder then'. (Mitch Hedberg)

Lies

If a writer says he doesn't read reviews of his work, his nose will grow longer and longer until eventually it falls off. (Hugh Leonard)

Life

Life is a moderately good play with a badly written third act. (Truman Capote)

Lillian Hellman
Every word Hellman wrote was a lie, including 'and' and 'the.' (Mary McCarthy)

Lolita
I haven't read *Lolita* yet. I'm waiting until she's 18. (Groucho Marx)

Longwindedness
Gertrude Stein was masterly in making nothing happen very slowly. (Clifton Fadiman)

I have the reputation for having read all of Henry James. Which would suggest a mis-spent youth *and* middle age. (James Thurber)

Lord Byron
Byron would have been forgotten today if he'd lived to be a florid old gentleman with iron-grey whiskers, writing very able letters to *The Times* about the repeal of corn laws. (Max Beerbohm)

Lost Generation
I have to laugh when I look back at those who called themselves the Lost Generation. All those poor idiots were moaning about were ants in the picnic basket. (Charles Bukowski)

Louis Auchincloss
Auchincloss is a second-rate Stephen Birmingham. And Birmingham is third-rate. (Truman Capote)

Love
If you want to read about love and marriage, buy two separate books. (Alan King)

We are all sick and can read only those books which treat our disease. This explains the success of love stories. (Jean Cocteau)

Love Letters
It is good to write love letters. There are certain things for which it is not easy to ask your mistress face to face. Like money, for instance. (Henri de Regnier)

James Hunt used to write me love letters from all over the world. Well not actually love letters. They were more like technical reports on his car. (Taormina Rich)

A woman's best love letters are always written to the man she's betraying. (Lawrence Durrell)

Ludwig Beethoven
I'm a great lover of Beethoven - especially the poems. (Ringo Starr)

M

Magazines
If Botticelli was alive today he'd be writing for *Vogue*. (Peter Ustinov)

Magazines are the heavy petting of literature. (Fran Lebowitz)

Malcolm Muggeridge
That garden gnome expelled from Eden has come to rest as a gargoyle brooding over a derelict cathedral. (Kenneth Tynan)

Manuscripts
When I get manuscripts from aspiring poets I do one of two things. If there's no stamped addressed envelope, I throw it into the bin. If there is, I write and tell them to fuck off. (Philip Larkin)

Thank you for your manuscript. I shall lose no time in reading it. (Benjamin Disraeli)

Marcel Proust
Rack my brains as I may, I can't see why a chap should need thirty pages to describe how he turns over in bed before going to sleep. (Marc Humbolt)

Marilyn Monroe
There are more books on Marilyn than there are on World War II, and I think there's a great similarity between them. (Billy Wilder)

Marriage
If you ever think you married the world's worst shit, you're wrong. I did. (Martha Gellhorn on Ernest Hemingway)

I find comfort in the fact that women do not stay married to Hemingway. (Alexander Woolcott)

It was very good of God to let Mr and Mrs Carlyle marry one another and so make only two people miserable instead of four. (Samuel Butler)

Masterpieces
The greatest literary masterpiece is just a dictionary out of order. (Jean Cocteau)

Cyril Connolly's lost masterpieces give a piquancy to his criticism, just as childless lovers make the best babysitters and impotent men the most assiduous lovers. (Malcolm Muggeridge)

While clearly an impregnable masterpiece, *Don Quixote* suffers from one fairly serious flaw - it's unreadable. (Martin Amis)

If I ever write a masterpiece it will be the result of a month in bed alone. (Siegfried Sassoon)

Matthew Arnold
Poor Matt, he's gone to heaven no doubt. But he won't like God. (Robert Louis Stevenson after Arnold died)

Meat
There was a time when I thought my only connection with the literary world would be that I once delivered meat to T.S. Eliot's mother-in-law. (Alan Bennett)

Meetings
Wanting to meet an author because you like his books is as ridiculous as wanting to meet a goose because you like *pate de foie gras*. (Arthur Koestler)

Melodrama
It makes *Mutiny on the Bounty* look like a United Free Church of Scotland choir outing on a hot June afternoon. (James T. Cameron on Alastair McLean's first novel, *HMS Ulysses*)

Memoirs
Bill Clinton is getting $8 million for his memoirs. Hillary got the same for hers. That's $16 million for two people who, for eight years, couldn't remember anything. (Jay Leno)

My brother Brian has just written his memoirs. Memoirs me arse. You could write that fellow's memoirs on the back of a stamp and still have enough room left for the Koran. (Brendan Behan)

Memorising
Any actor who tries to memorise a David Mamet play eventually wants to commit suicide. (William Macy)

Menus
I hate reading. Someone just tell me what's on the menu! (Paris Hilton)

Metre
I hate loose metre even more than loose women. (William Inge)

Mill on the Floss
The man who said the pen is mightier than the sword should have tried reading *The Mill on the Floss* to a group of motor mechanics. (Tom Sharpe)

Minimalism
The best scene I ever wrote in a film was when a girl said 'Uh-huh' three times. (Raymond Chandler)

'Yes,' he said, succinctly. (Danielle Steele)

Mirrors

A book is a mirror. If an ass peers into it, you can't expect an apostle to look out. (Georg Lichtenberg)

Misconceptions

I'm the kind of writer people think other people are reading. (V. S. Naipaul)

Mistakes

I was very frank about myself in my autobiography. I told about my first mistake on Page 850. (Henry Kissinger)

Mobile Libraries

I was knocked down by a mobile library once. I was lying in the middle of the road screaming in agony. Then the driver got out and said, 'Shhh.' (Jimmy Cricket)

Modernity

If you say a modern celebrity is an adulterer, a pervert and a drug addict, all it means is that you've read his autobiography. (P.J. O'Rourke)

Today's literature: prescriptions written by patients. (Karl Kraus)

Molly Irvins
Irvins delivers laidback wisdom with the serenity of a downhome Buddha who's just discovered stool softeners really work. (Florynce King)

Mothers
My mother just wrote her autobiography. It's entitled 'I Came, I Saw, I Criticised'. (Judy Gold)

Motivation
I write my books because I need to know what's inside them. (Julian Green)

I began writing for the simple reason that the days in winter were short, the evenings long, and after the logs had been split, the sheep seen to, the mowers covered and the hay gathered, there was nothing to do. (Dirk Bogarde)

Write to amuse? What an appalling suggestion. I write to make people anxious and miserable and to worsen their indigestion. (Wendy Cope)

Perhaps it is only desperation which keeps me writing, like someone who clings on to an unhappy marriage for fear of solitude. (Graham Greene)

Movies
Having your book turned into a movie is like seeing oxen turned into bouillon cubes. (John Le Carré)

Death Wish came from a novella by a writer called Brian Garfield. I think it sold three copies. Brian's mother bought two of them. (Michael Winner)

Multi-Tasking
People sometimes ask me if I multi-task. I tell them I do. I read in the bathroom. (Jo Brand)

Murder
Murder in literature is considered less immoral than fornication. (George Moore)

My brother-in-law once wrote an unusual murder story. The victim got killed by a man from another book. (Robert Sylvester)

A guy tried to pick me up in a bookstore by recommending books to me. He found a murder mystery and wrote his phone number on it. I called him and said, 'I didn't like the book but now I know how to kill you. This call is coming from inside your house.' (Daryl Hogue)

When we want to read of the deeds that are done for love, whither do we turn? To the murder column. (George Bernard Shaw)

Music
Music journalism is people who can't write interviewing people who can't talk for people who can't read. (Frank Zappa)

N

Names
I was named after a necrophiliac drug addicted sadomasochistic latent homosexual. (E.L. Doctorow - he was referring to Edgar Allan Poe)

Evelyn Waugh was a misanthrope. He could be excused because he never got over having been christened with a girl's name. If a man called Evelyn is reading this he'll probably hit me with his hockey stick. (Hugh Leonard)

Nappies
Like many women, I can't understand why every man who has ever changed a nappy has felt impelled, in recent years, to write a book about it. (Barbara Ehrenreich)

National Enquirer
Thank God I'm low enough on the totem pole that *The National Enquirer* doesn't fuck with me. (Charles Bukowski)

News
No news is good news. No journalists, even better. (Nicholas Bentley)

How is it that there's always just enough news in newspapers to fill the pages? (Don Peterson)

It's wonderful how much news there is when people write every other day. If they wait for a month, though, there's nothing that's worth telling. (O. Douglas)

Newspapers
The papers are full of the atomic bomb, which is going to blow us all to buggery. Not a bad idea. (Noel Coward)

What paper does he write for? (Yogi Berra after being asked if he knew Ernest Hemingway)

The only thing you can believe in a newspaper is the date. (J.B.S. Haldane)

Newspaper Editors
After a marriage lasting only seven days, a newspaper editor's wife has filed a petition for divorce on the grounds that he is too small a type, she's become bored with his special features and he refuses to give her a late-night extra. (The Two Ronnies)

Newspaper Owners
In my time in Fleet Street I often felt that newspaper owners would be much happier if they didn't have to employ awkward people like journalists. (Barry Norman)

New Testament
The New Testament isn't new anymore. It's thousands of years old. It's time for us to start calling it The Less Old Testament. (George Carlin)

Noses
I always had my nose in a book when I was growing up. We couldn't afford Kleenex. (Joe Hickman)

Novels
All novels should have a beginning, a muddle and an end. (Philip Larkin)

I'm writing a novel about a one-legged psychopath who rapes his mother, murders his father and then falls in love with a duckbilled platypus from Mars. It's based on fact. (Daniel Grovier)

Monica Baldwin's book *I Leap Over the Wall* was very interesting. I must say it has strengthened my decision not to become a nun. (Noel Coward)

An American novel is a story in which two people want each other from the beginning but don't get each other until the end. A French novel is a story in which two people get together at the beginning but from then until the end they don't want each other any more. A Russian novel is a story in which the two people don't want *or* get each other and brood about he fact for 800 pages. (Erich Maria Remarque).

Russian novels go on for about 942 pages. On page 920 Boris the peasant decides he wants to commit suicide. After he's topped himself you find yourself wishing he did it on page 4. (Frank McCourt)

If you nail anything down in a novel either it kills it or the novel gets up and walks away with the nail. (D.H. Laurence)

I'm sick and tired of novelists who write novels about novelists writing novels about novelists. (John Broderick)

O

Obstacles
The biggest obstacle to professional writing today is the necessity of changing a typewriter ribbon. (Robert Benchley)

Oh Calcutta
Oh Calcutta is the kind of show that gives pornography a bad name. (Clive Barnes)

Old Testament
The Old Testament is about prophet and lust. (Colin Bowles)

On the Road
Kerouac's book isn't writing. It's just typing. (Truman Capote)man who, when he said a good thing, knew nobody had said it before him. (Mark Twain)

Outer Space
America has spent millions of dollars trying to develop a pen that can write in outer space. The Russians are smarter than us. They use pencils. (Leo McGarry)

Oxymorons

An oxymoron is a contradiction in terms, as when we say something like 'The witty Jane Austen.' (Patrick Murray)

P

Pages

I'm writing a book. I've got the page numbers done already. (Steven Wright)

Whenever anyone recommends a book to me by saying 'It's a page-turner' I say, 'Yes, I know how the things works.' (Jimmy Carr)

Pain

The more shit a man swims in, the better the keys bite into the paper. (Charles Bukowski)

Paperbacks

The paperback is very interesting but it will never replace a hardcover book as it makes such a poor doorstop. (Alfred Hitchcock)

Paradise Lost

Milton wrote *Paradise Lost*. Then his wife died and he wrote *Paradise Regained*. (Frank Muir)

Parties

A literary party is a traffic jam of the lost waiting for a ferry across the Styx. (Delmore Schwartz)

Christy Brown partied so much after the publication of *Down All the Days* it should really have been called *Up All the Nights*. (Georgina Hambleton)

Passion
No passion in the world is equal to the passion to alter someone else's draft. (H.G. Wells)

Passive Voice
The Passive Voice should never be used. (William Safire)

Pencils
Have you got a pencil? I left my typewriter in my other pants. (Groucho Marx)

Pens
The pen is mightier than the sword - and considerably easier to write with. (Marty Feldman)

No man was more foolish when he had not a pen in his hand, nor more wise when he had. (Dr Johnson on Oliver Goldsmith)

I've always wanted to write a book but I don't have a pen. (Tom Baker)

Pen Names
I wrote a book under a pen name. Bic. (Buzz Nutley)

I would venture to guess that 'Anon', who wrote so many poems without signing them, was often a woman. (Virginia Woolf)

Percy Bysshe Shelley
Shelley's poetry shouldn't be read; it should be inhaled through a gas pipe. (Lionel Trilling)

If Shelley had been anything of a gardener he would have known that spring is invariably far behind. (Spike Hughes)

Permanence
I never did anything more permanent than a popcorn fart in a typhoon. (James Michener)

Photographs
I hate book jacket photographs that don't do writers justice. Or ones that do them too much justice, so that when you meet them you get a fright. (Mitchell Symons)

Phone Books
It was a great moment for me when I realised the phone book was alphabetical. It took hours off looking up numbers. (Karl Spain)

I read a book recently that had too many characters and no plot. When I brought it back to the library they said, 'Why did you steal the phone book?' (Dorothy Fraser)

Plagiarism
Anticipator plagiarism occurs when someone steals your idea and publishes it 100 years before you were born. (Robert Merton)

Playboy
A woman reading *Playboy* is like a Jew reading a Nazi manual. (Gloria Steinem)

I hear *Playboy* is laying off 8% of the workforce. That would be the guy who writes the articles. (Jay Leno)

My boyfriend used to say he read *Playboy* for the articles. Right. And I go to the malls for the music. (Rita Rudner)

Playwrights
The first rule for a young playwright is not to write like Henry Arthur Jones. The second and third rules are the same. (Oscar Wilde)

By increasing the size of the keyhole, today's playwrights are in danger of doing away with the door. (Peter Ustinov)

Playwrights only puts down what we says and then charges us to hear it. (Denis Murphy)

If a playwright is funny, the English look for the serious message. If he's serious they look for the joke. (Sacha Guitry)

Plays

It's easy to write a play. You sit in front of a page where there are two characters and one of them would want to say something pretty fast. (Hugh Leonard)

I didn't like the play but then I saw it under adverse conditions. The curtain was up. (Groucho Marx)

It has taken 33 years for Jean-Paul Sartre's *The Devil and the Good Lord* to reach London. Our luck was bound to run out sooner or later. (Kenneth Hurren)

During the performance of the play I leaned forward and politely asked the lady in front of me if she would mind putting on her hat. (George S. Kaufman)

Its impact was like the banging together of two damp dishcloths. (Brendan Behan)

The play had only one fault. It was kind of lousy. (James Thurber)

Plots

When a plot flags, bring in a man with a gun. (Raymond Chandler)

This book has too much plot and not enough story. (Sam Goldwyn)

Plumbers
A good plumber is much more valuable than a good writer. (Charles Bukowski)

Poetry
When one looks at the progress of post-war English poetry it's like watching a dinosaur take side-steps in wet concrete. (Jeremy Reed)

Poetry isn't a career. It's a mug's game. No honest poet can ever feel quite sure if he has messed up his life for nothing. (T.S. Eliot)

Poetry sections are usually put in the back of bookshops, like pornography. (Desmond Clarke)

Rod McKuen's poetry isn't even trash. (Karl Shapiro)

Poets
Show me a poet and I'll show you a shit. (A.J. Liebling)

Watching large poets work with miniaturist forms can be a bit disorienting - like meeting a heavyweight fighter out walking a chihuahua. (Blake Morrison)

Poets, like whores, are only hated by each other. (William Wycherley)

You don't have to write to be a poet. Some people work in gas stations and they're poets. I don't call myself a poet because I don't like the word. I'm a trapeze artist. (Bob Dylan)

Popularity
May Sarton's lack of popularity is due to her habit of dissecting her bowels and displaying them for public observation. (*Maine Life*)

Alexander Solzenitsyn is a bad novelist and a fool. The combination usually makes for great popularity in the U.S. (Gore Vidal)

Books for general reading always smell badly. The odour of common people hangs about them. (Friedrich Nietzsche)

Pornography
I hate to think of this sort of book getting into the wrong hands. As soon as I've finished it, I shall recommend they ban it. (Tony Hancock on a pornographic novel he was reading)

Positive Thinking
I was going to buy a book called *The Power of Positive Thinking* but then I thought: What the hell good would that do? (Ronnie Shakes)

I was enjoying a book I was reading on positive thinking until I heard the author had committed suicide. (Nick Job)

Possession

The possession of a book often becomes a substitute for not reading it. (Anthony Burgess)

Posterity
Posterity is what you write for when you've been turned down by all the best publishers. (George Ade)

Why should we do anything for posterity? What's posterity ever done for us? (Sir Boyle Roche)

Your works will be read after Shakespeare and Milton are forgotten... but not *until* then. (English classicist Richard Porson to poet Robert Southey)

Postscripts
A woman seldom writes what's on her mind but in her postscript. (Richard Steele)

Poverty
I never knew a man who played *Hamlet* that didn't die broke. (Humphrey Bogart)

Praise
One always tend to over-praise a big book because one has been through it. (E.M. Forster)

Predictions
The day will come when books will be sold by weight, like soap, and bear the same relationship to literature as a packet of detergent. (John Broderick)

Prefaces
Shaw's plays are the price we pay for his Prefaces. (James Agate)

Preferences
I'd rather be a great bad poet than a good bad poet. (Ogden Nash)

I'd rather win a water fight in a swimming pool than write The Great American Novel. (Jack London)

I know a lot of writers but I prefer people. (Malcolm Bradbury)

Japanese kabuki theatre is barely preferable to root canal work. (A.A. Gill)

Pregnancy
Women write novels to while away their pregnancies. (W. Somerset Maugham)

Prepositions
A preposition is something you should never end a sentence with. (Beryl Bainbridge)

Press Men
If I was the local milkman, or some poor cunt flogging turf from the back of a donkey's cart, the whores wouldn't even stop to give me a light. (Brendan Behan)

Priorities
The first thing a writer has to do is find another source of income. (Ellen Gilchrist)

Books used to call for pen, ink and a writing desk. Today the rule is that a pen, ink and a writing desk call for a book. (Friedrich Nietzsche)

Prison
They sent Oscar Wilde to prison for doing what writers today get knighted for. (Wilfrid Hyde-White)

Prizes
The Nobel Prize is a ticket to one's own funeral. No one has ever done anything after he got it. (T.S. Eliot)

Progress
What progress we're making. In the Middle Ages they would have burned me at the stake. Now they're content with burning my books. (Sigmund Freud)

Promiscuity
My wife recently told a not-very-bookish friend of hers that she was reading a Trollope. 'Which one,' came the reply, 'Jackie Collins?' (Craig Brown)

Proofs
I worked all morning on the proofs of one of my poems and did nothing but take out a comma. In the afternoon I put it back in. (Oscar Wilde)

The day a writer corrects his first set of proofs he's as proud as a schoolboy who's just got his first dose of the pox. (Charles Baudelaire)

Publication
His book hit the world with all the impact of a feather falling onto a piece of damp blotting-paper. (Patrick Moore)

For those of you who haven't read the book, it's being published tomorrow. (David Frost)

Publicity
Every writer ought to have at least one thing he does well. Truman Capote's gift for publicity is the most glittering star in his diadem. (Gore Vidal)

There's no such thing as bad publicity except your obituary. (Brendan Behan)

Public Readings
To read your work in public is a kind of mental incest. (Stephen Behan)

I've never stooped so low as to sleep with a poet but I attend Poetry Society readings. There you'll spot a dozen intense young women in lumpen cardigans trying to seduce a man with dandruff. (Rowan Pelling)

Publishers
I have never caught a publisher working. (J.B. Priestly)

Just as repressed sadists are supposed to become policemen or butchers, so those with an irrational fear of life become publishers. (Cyril Connolly)

A publisher who writes is like a cow in a milk bar. (Arthur Koestler)

I'm always wary of intellectual publishers. They offer you patronage instead of hard cash and swear by high heaven to make you famous by the time you've spent your first decade in eternity. (Christy Brown)

One of the great signs of Napoleon's greatness is the fact that he once had a publisher shot. (Siegfried Unseld)

Barabbas was a publisher. (Thomas Campbell)

Publishing
Publish and be damned. (Duke of Wellington)

Publish and be sued. (Richard Ingrams)

Pubs
Shakespeare went into a pub once but was told,
'Get out, you're barred.' (Peter Kay)

Q

Qualifications
The chief qualification to be a poet is that one be born. (H.H. Munro)

Questions
My publisher sent me a questionnaire to fill in about myself in order to help sales of my book in Norway. Under 'Hobbies' I listed 'Tattooing snakes on sailors' bottoms.' (Evelyn Waugh)

Is there no beginning to your talents? (Clive Anderson to Jeffrey Archer in 1991)

Anne Robinson: 'Complete the title of the Jerome K. Jerome book *Three Men in a...*'
Contestant: '*Baby.*'
(The Weakest Link)

Quotations
Don't quote from the classics. That's like digging up your grandmother in front of your mistress. (Leon-Paul- Fargue)

My car broke down so I took it to the garage and asked the mechanic for a quotation. He said, 'To be or not to be.' (Les Dawson)

Hamlet is an okay play but there are too many quotations in it. (Milton Berle)

R

Races

If Seamus Heaney belonged to an unfashionable race, were he a Welshman for instance, his poetry would have been lucky to make it into the parish magazine. (A.N. Wilson)

Ralph Waldo Emerson

Waldo Emerson is one of those people who would be enormously improved by death. (Saki)

I called him a wrinkled and toothless baboon, a man who was first hoisted in notoriety on the shoulders of Carlyle and who now spits and splutters on a filthier platform of his own finding and fouling. (Algernon Charles Swinburne)

Ransom

The only way you'll make money from writing is by composing ransom notes. (Jackie Mason)

Readability

Carlyle's *Sartor Resartus* is unreadable. To me that always sort of spoils a book. (Will Cuppy)

Readers

I've now written seven books, which isn't bad for someone who's only read three. (George Burns)

I don't read everything I read in the press. (Dave Jones)

I've read part of your book all the way through. (Sam Goldwyn)

Reader's Digest
I write for *The Reader's Digest*. It's not hard. All you do is copy out an article and mail it in again. (Milt Kamen)

Reading
I've given up reading books. I find it takes my mind off myself. (Oscar Levant)

Really? What is she reading? (Dame Edith Evans after being told Nancy Mitford was about to finish a book)

I never was much on this book-reading. It takes 'em too long to describe the eye colour of all the characters. (Will Rogers)

All my best and most enjoyable reading was done in the lavatory. (Henry Miller)

My favourite writers are Joyce, Tolstoy, Proust and Flaubert but right now I'm reading *The Little Ship That Could*. (Emo Philips)

A great many people now reading and writing would be better employed in keeping rabbits. (Dame Edith Sitwell)

103

Rebels
In the Soviet Union a writer who's critical of the establishment is taken to a lunatic asylum. In America he's taken to a talk show. (Carlos Fuentes)

Records
In the restricted space of two-thirds of a page of *Deerslayer*, James Fenimore Cooper has scored 114 offences against literary art out of a possible 115. It breaks the record. (Mark Twain)

Recycling
Danielle Steele's *Message From Nam* is a work without any redeeming value unless it can be recycled as a cardboard box. (Ellen Goodman)

Rejection
My dear sir, I have read your play. Oh, my dear sir. (Herbert Beerbohm Tree to a prospective author)

Seventeen publishers rejected the manuscript, at which time we knew we had something hot. (Kinky Friedman)

I have the ultimate rejection slip. The publishers burned my manuscript and sent me the ashes. (Mike Lanford)

Relaxation
I'm trying to read a book on how to relax but it's boring me. I keep falling asleep. (Jim Loy)

Repetition
Horatio Alger wrote the same novel 135 times. (George Juergens)

Waiting for Godot is a play in which nothing happens twice. (Hugh Kenner)

Reporters
I always warn aspiring reporters to observe three basic rules: 1. Never trust an editor. 2. Never trust an editor. 3. Never trust an editor. (Edna Buchanan)

Reputations
Max Beerbohm is the only author whose reputation increases with every book he *doesn't* publish. (W. Somerset Maugham)

Make the reader laugh and he will think you a trivial fellow. Bore him in the right way and your reputation is assured. (Somerset Maugham)

If you live long enough your reputation will die twice. (Robert Lowell)

Research

I do a great deal of research for my writing, especially in the apartments of tall blondes. (Raymond Chandler)

Resignation

I was blessed with a crappy life. (Charles Bukowski)

Retirement

We always wonder why a writer stops writing. I sometimes think we should wonder more at the ones who don't. (Lawrence Block)

Stephen King has written a letter to his fans saying he's repeating himself too much and is going to retire from writing novels. The letter is 500 pages long and ends with a bucket of blood being tossed into a possessed car. (Craig Kilborn)

Revelations

Some men kiss and tell. George Moore tells but he doesn't kiss. (Sarah Purser)

Reviews

One cannot review a bad book without showing off. (W.H. Auden)

I never read a book before reviewing it. It prejudices one so. (Sydney Smyth)

Book reviewers are little old ladies of both sexes. (John O'Hara)

Once, while reviewing a terrible production of Shaw's *Androcles and the Lion* where the actors seemed to be in three different plays, I concentrated most of my review on the actor who played the lion. He had no lines but he clearly knew what Shaw wanted. And his mime was delicious. (Ben Pleasants)

A bad review is less important than whether it's raining in Patagonia. (Iris Murdoch)

Rewinding
The big advantage of a book is that it's very easy to rewind. Close it and you're right back at the beginning. (Jerry Seinfeld)

Re-Writing
If it looks like writing I re-write it. (Elmore Leonard)

Richard Burton
Burton was so vigorous and healthy when he played *Hamlet* I can honestly say it was the only version of the play in which the audience felt sorry for Claudius. (Oscar Levant)

Robert Browning
Browning uses words with the violence of a horse-breaker giving out the scent of a she-goat. (Ford Madox Ford)

Robert Louis Stevenson
I think of him as a consumptive youth weaving garlands of sad flowers with pale, weak hands. (George Moore)

Romeo and Juliet
Romeo and Juliet only spent one night together. The following day Romeo committed suicide. Then Juliet committed suicide. I'm trying to find out what went on in that bedroom. (Alan King)

Royalties
If the queen wrote a book, would she get royalties? (Mitch Lawlor)

Rules
There are three rules for writing novels. Unfortunately, nobody knows what they are. (W. Somerset Maugham)

Where I work we have only one editorial rule. We can't write anything longer than the average person can read during the average crap. (Jeff Goldblum in *The Big Chill*)

S

Sacrifice
Mauriac, Gide and Julien Green - you wouldn't think Jesus Christ died for those miserable bastards, would you? (Roy Campbell)

Saints
When John McGahern died he was like a secular saint. That guy taught me in Belgrove. At the time I just saw him as a teacher who wrote. Now he's like Padre Pio. (Neil Jordan)

Sales
My books are selling like wildfire. Everyone's burning them. (Lee Dunne)

A good bishop, denouncing a book from the pulpit with the right organ note in his voice can add between fifteen and twenty thousand to the sales. (P.G. Wodehouse)

Samuel Beckett
Beckett's work is a mansend for academics and the intellectual elite. For the former it provides an infinity of thesis fodder. For the latter it serves as a bludgeon with which to clobber their supposed inferiors. (Con Houlihan)

Beckett's plays remind me of something John Betjeman might do if you filled him up with benzedrine and then force-fed him intravenously with Guinness. (Tom Davies)

Life is hard enough without having to read Beckett. (Brian Behan)

Scoops
If there's one thing better than breaking a great scoop, it's exposing a rival's great scoop as a fake. (Piers Morgan)

Seamus O'Sullivan
The only trouble with O'Sullivan is that when he's not drunk he's sober. (W.B. Yeats)

Self-Help Books
I once bought a self-help book. It was so complicated I had to get someone to help me read it. (Jackie Vernon)

I went to a bookstore and asked the saleswoman, 'Where's the self-help section?' She said if she told me it would defeat the purpose. (George Carlin)

Self-Image
As a writer, I'm nothing more than a perfect sausage machine. (Agatha Christie)

I'm an alcoholic. I'm a drug addict. I'm a homosexual. I'm a genius. (Truman Capote)

Selfishness
I write for myself and strangers. The strangers, dear readers, are an afterthought. (Gertrude Stein)

Sequels
I'm writing a sequel to *The Da Vinci Code*. It's called *I Know What You Did Last Supper*. (Paul Lyalls)

Sequels add a new terror to the deaths of novelists. (Peter Ackroyd)

Sex
I bought my wife a sex manual but half the pages were missing. It meant we went straight from foreplay to post-natal depression. (Bob Monkhouse)

I've written every possible kind of sex scene except a couple doing it standing up in a hammock. (Lee Dunne)

Murder is a crime but writing about it isn't. Sex isn't a crime but writing about it is. (Larry Flynt)

Edmund Wilson was a fat bore who made fornication as dull as a railroad timetable. (Raymond Chandler)

Sheep
Wordsworth was a half-witted sheep who bleated articulate monotony. (James Stephens)

Short Stories
The most famous Irish short story, 'The Dead', is famous for, among other things, not being very short. (Frank McNally)

Significance
Albert Camus won the Nobel Prize for his novel *The Outsider* which says, in effect, that life is meaningless. The novel's dust jacket reported that Camus died in a car wreck in 1960. It should have added, 'Not that it matters'. (Dexter Madison)

Silence
I could not have gone on through the awful wretched mess of my life without having left a stain upon the silence. (Samuel Beckett)

Size
The three smallest books in the world are the *British Book of Space Achievers*, *Italian War Heroes* and the *Scottish Giftbook*. (Robert McKee)

Sleep
I fell asleep reading a dull book. I dreamt that I was reading on so I awoke from sheer boredom. (Heinrich Heine)

Slogans
I think your slogan 'Liberty or Death' is splendid. Whichever one you decide on will be all right with me. (Alexander Woolcott to Harold Ross, editor of the *New Yorker*)

Snakes
Evil is perversely compelling. *The Bible* is duller than the operating instructions for a hinge until the snake shows up. (Dennis Miller)

Sneezing
I like to write when I feel spiteful. It's like having a good sneeze. (D.H. Lawrence)

Socrates
The more I read him, the less I wonder why they poisoned him. (Thomas Babington Macaulay)

Soldiers
Ernest Hemingway thought of himself as a soldier. He wasn't. He was just a tourist in a helmet. (Charles Whiting)

Songs
If I can sing it, it's a song. If I can't, it's a poem (Bob Dylan)

I can't remember if I was awake or asleep when I wrote *Streams of Whiskey*. (Shane MacGowan)

Sons
During the blitz I was asked if I wanted my books or my son evacuated to safety. I chose the books because many of them were irreplaceable. I knew I could always have another son. (Evelyn Waugh)

Speech
The earliest example of a talking child in *The Bible* is when Job cursed the day he was born. (Niall Toibin)

Speed Reading
I've taken up speed-reading. I can read *War and Peace* in two seconds now. Okay, so it's only three words but it's a start. (Tim Vine)

Stains
If I peed on paper they'd print the stain. (Germaine Greer)

Statues
Have you ever seen a statue erected to a critic? (John Steinbeck)

Stephen Spender
One watches Stephen Spender use the English language with the same horrified fascination as watching a Sevres vase in the hands of a chimpanzee. (Evelyn Waugh)

Stereotyping
A lot of people think they can take my books and analyse me from them. On that principle Agatha Christie would be a serial killer. (Muriel Spark)

Subject Matter
Henry James turned his back on one of the great events in the world's history, the rise of the United States, in order to report tittle-tattle at tea parties in English country houses. (Somerset Maugham)

Subways
I was on the subway sitting on a newspaper. A guy comes over and asks, 'Are you reading that?' I didn't know what to say so I said, 'Yes.' Then I stood up, turned the page, and sat down again. (David Brenner)

Success
A book is a success when people who haven't read it pretend they have. (*Los Angeles Times*)

For a writer, success is only delayed failure. (Graham Greene)

A successful poetry book is any one that sells more than four copies in a given store. (Michael Wiegers)

A good poem about failure is a success. (Philip Larkin)

Suffering

It's an old theory that you have to suffer in order to write but I dislike it. I'd rather be happy and never write. (Charles Bukowski)

Suicide

I hope he goes out and hangs himself as soon as possible. (Ernest Hemingway on James Jones after the publication of *From Here to Eternity*)

Nobody ever committed suicide while reading a good book but many have while trying to write one. (Robert Byrne)

Survival

Getting hitched up to a rich woman is about the only way a poet can keep up an adequate supply of whisky for himself. (Patrick Kavanagh)

Synonyms

A synonym is a word you use when you can't spell the other one. (Baltasar Gracian)

Is there any other word for synonym? (Paul Cryer)

T

Talent
Having no talent is no longer enough to become a success. (Gore Vidal)

Targets
The main target of my books lies somewhere between the solar plexus and the upper thigh. (Ian Fleming)

Tattoos
To many people, dramatic criticism must seem like an attempt to tattoo soap bubbles. (John Mason Brown)

Writing is an engraving of pain, a tattooing of myself. (Anais Nin)

Tax
I once asked Alun Owen what the tax advantages of living in Ireland were for a writer. 'None,' he said, 'What you save on tax you spend on drink'. (Spike Milligan)

Writer's block is so bad with me these days, the only fiction I'm writing is my tax returns. (Alan Morrissey)

Tea

It says in the Bible that a man should always make the tea. It's in Hebrews. (Greg Knight)

Ted Hughes

Ted Hughes has been more pissed on than the back wall of the Batley Working Men's Club before a Dusty Springfield concert. (Alan Bennett)

T.E. Lawrence

Lawrence had a genius for backing into the limelight. (Lowell Thomas)

Television

TV has raised writing to a new low. (Samuel Goldwyn)

I saw *Under Milk Wood* on TV. The best thing in the programme was the 20 minute breakdown. (George Murray)

Adapting *Middlemarch* for television is like getting an elephant into a suitcase. (Andrew Davies)

Tennessee Williams

If a swamp alligator could talk, it would sound like Williams. (Rex Reed)

Theatre
The only good thing about the theatre is that you can leave at the interval. (Philip Larkin)

Long experience has taught me that in England nobody goes to the theatre unless he has bronchitis. (James Agate)

I don't go to the theatre to see plays about rape, sodomy and drug addiction. I can get that at home. (Peter Cook)

The only thing I ever got from the theatre was a sore arse. (Paul McCartney)

It's one of the tragic ironies of the theatre that only one man in it can count on steady work - the night watchman. (Tallulah Bankhead)

There was laughter at the back of the theatre, leading to the belief that someone was telling jokes back there. (George S. Kaufman on a comedy he attended)

Theft
I once stole a pornographic book that was printed in Braille. I used to rub the dirty parts. (Woody Allen)

Thomas Gray
Gray walks as if he'd fouled his clothes – and *looks* as if he smelt it. (Christopher Smart)

119

Thomas Wolfe

To hell with Tom Wolfe. I shit on his grave. He drivels his jacked-up juvenile romantic cockism all up and down the pages, wearing you out like a pair of stockings. (Charles Bukowski)

Thomas Woolfe was a one-book glandular giant with the guts of three mice. (Ernest Hemingway)

Threats

If you write anything nasty about me I'll come round and blow up your toilet. (Courtney Love to a journalist)

Time

Where do I find the time for not reading so many books? (Karl Kraus)

In the old days books were written by men of letters and read by the public. Nowadays they're written by the public and read by nobody. (Oscar Wilde)

Titles

I want to write a best-seller so I've decided to call it *Harry Potter and the Da Vinci Code of Sudoko*. (David O'Doherty)

It should have been called *The Bridges of Menopause County*. (Brush Sheils on *The Bridges of Madison County*)

Stephen King has just written a horror book called *It*. How can that sell? 'Honey – there's a pronoun in the basement!' (Richard Pryor)

Anne Robinson: 'Complete the title of the play *The Iceman...*
Contestant: '*Melts*.'
(The Weakest Link)

Tours
Writers today go on autographing tours as a matter of course. They talk at book fairs. They're occasionally photographed as Men of Distinction holding a glass of blended whiskey that I should be almost afraid to pour down the drains for fear of corroding the metal. (Raymond Chandler)

Translations
I'm the most translated author in the world behind Lenin, Tolstoy, Gorki and Jules Verne. And they're all dead. (Mickey Spillane)

He'd been a precocious child, an intellectual. At twelve, without help, he'd managed to translate the complete works of T.S. Eliot into English. (Woody Allen)

Trash
A bit of trash now and then is good for the severest reader. It provides the necessary roughage in the literary diet. (Phyllis McGinley)

Travel Writing
Most travel books are written by people whose only talent is for travel. (John Broderick)

I always thought I'd like to be a travel writer. The problem was, I never went anywhere. And I can't write. (Ellen DeGeneres)

Trilogies
I'm writing an Irish trilogy. It has four books in it. (Brendan O'Carroll)

Truman Capote
People judge Capote too charitably when they refer to him as a child. He's more like a sweetly vicious old lady. (Tennessee Williams)

Truth
Autobiographies are unrivalled vehicles for telling the truth about others. (Philip Guedalla)

Poetry is truth in its Sunday clothes. (Joseph Roux)

T.S. Eliot
'The Cocktail Party', or rather the cocktale farty, struck me as little more than stale gobbets of auden-isherwood boiled up in 'mysticism' on the grgr (Graham Greene) level. (Kingsley Amis)

Eliot has arrived at the supreme eminence of English critics largely through disguising himself as a corpse. (Ezra Pound)

Eliot's face had deep lines. I wish I could say the same for his poetry. (Melville Cane)

Turnips
If only they'd talk about turnips. (James Joyce to Samuel Beckett when listening to a group of people discussing literature at a party)

Typewriters
I know so little about typewriters, I once bought a new one because I couldn't change the ribbon on the one I had. (Dorothy Parker)

Some poetry seems to have been written on typewriters by other typewriters. (Randall Jarrell)

Typing
What would I do if I had only six months to live? I'd type faster. (Irving Berlin)

I can always find plenty of women to sleep with me. The kind of one that's really hard to find is a typist who can read my writing. (Thomas Wolfe)

U

Ulysses
In Ireland they try to make a cat clean by rubbing its nose in its own filth. Mr Joyce has tried the same treatment on the human subject. (George Bernard Shaw)

Uncles
A great uncle of my wife's once felt it necessary to emigrate to India because he had failed to return a long overdue library book. (Dannie Abse)

Understanding
My son writes poetry. I know it's good because I can't understand a word of it. (Eliza Goodge)

There have been a couple of books written about me by critics. I don't read them because I don't want to know what my work is about. (Alan Bennett)

I live in terror of not being misunderstood. (Oscar Wilde)

Universities
Everywhere I go I'm asked if universities stifle writers. My opinion is that they don't stifle half enough of them. (Flannery O'Connor)

Unpopularity
Having been unpopular in high school is not just cause for book publications. (Fran Lebowitz)

Unpunctuality
Sorry my article is late. Too fucking busy. Or vice versa. (Dorothy Parker to an editor)

Unputdownability
Once you put a Henry James book down, there's no way you can pick it up again. (Mark Twain)

V

Valley of the Dolls
This is a book for the reader who has put away comics but is not yet ready for editorials in the *Daily News*. (Gloria Steinem)

Vanity
Lord Byron was always looking at himself in mirrors to make sure he was sufficiently outrageous. (Enoch Powell)

Victor Hugo
Victor Hugo was a madman who thought he was Victor Hugo. (Jean Cocteau)

Vita Sackville-West
Vita Sackville-West looked like Lady Chatterley above the waist and the gamekeeper below it. (Cyril Connolly)

Vocabulary
I don't think I'll ever write a book. The only big work I know is 'delicatessen.' And I can't spell it. (Lloyd Mangrum)

Walt Whitman laid end to end words never seen in each other's company before outside of a dictionary. (David Lodge)

Never use a long word when a diminutive one will do. (William Safire)

'Always' and 'never' are two words that you always should remember never to use. (Wendel Johnson)

Voices
Truman Capote's voice was so high it could only be detected by a bat. (Tennessee Williams)

Voyeurism
I read about authors' lives with the fascination of one slowing down to get a good look at an automobile accident. (Kaye Gibbons)

W

Waiting for Godot

I've been brooding in my bath and it is my considered opinion that the success of *Waiting for Godot* is the end of the theatre as we know it. (Robert Morley)

War

Without war Hemingway would have been a wine-drinking, pink-eyed picador for a fat and farting matador. It gave him the golden gate to point up some fairytale about guts for the cockeyed bats of the occident. (Charles Bukowski)

I spent twenty years perfecting the use of the colon. Then the war came. (Charles Morgan)

Warren Harding

Harding writes the worst English I have ever encountered. It reminds me of a string of wet sponges. It reminds me of tattered washing on the line. It reminds me of stale bean soup, of college yells, of dogs barking idiotically through endless nights. It is so bad that a sort of grandeur creeps into it. It drags itself out of the dark abysm of pish and crawls insanely up to the topmost pinnacle of posh. (H.L. Mencken)

Warren Report
At the moment I'm working on a non-fiction version of the Warren Report. (Woody Allen)

Weapons
I'm all in favour of keeping dangerous weapons out of the hands of fools. Let's start with typewriters. (Thomas Berger)

As I write this letter I have a pistol in one hand and a sword in the other. (Sir Boyle Roche)

W.H. Auden
Auden didn't love God; he just fancied him. (Michael Harkness)

Whodunits
I read a whodunit recently. It was the author. (Ronald Seltzer)

I peeked at the end of the Bible. The Devil did it. (John McIntyre)

I've just been reading the dictionary. It turns out the zebra did it. (Steven Wright)

William Butler Yeats
Yeats has reached the age where he won't take yes for an answer. (Oliver St. John Gogarty)

One should not look to poets for handy hints. W.B. Yeats had trouble walking properly, let alone boiling an egg without cracking it. (Craig Brown)

William Conrad

One of the surest signs of Conrad's genius is that women dislike his works. (George Orwell)

William Faulkner

I can never tell whether his characters are making love or playing tennis. (Joseph Kraft)

Faulkner's sentences run from here to the airport. (Carolyn Chute)

I knew William Faulkner very well. He was a great friend of mine. Well, as much as you could be a friend of his if you weren't a 14-year-old nymphet. (Truman Capote)

William Shakespeare

My father adored Shakespeare. Every time he caught sight of me he'd say, 'Is execution done on Cawdor?' That's question a pretty tough question when you're four. (John Mortimer)

Shakespeare wrote of the Seven Ages of Man but he didn't write of the Seven Ages of Women. That's because he couldn't find an age that any woman would admit to. (F.J. Mills)

We've all heard that a million monkeys banging on a million typewriters will eventually reproduce the entire works of Shakespeare. Now, thanks to the internet, we know that this not true. (Robert Wilensky)

With the single exception of Homer, there is no eminent writer, not even Sir Walter Scott, whom I despise so entirely as I despise Shakespeare when I measure my mind again his. It would positively be a relief to dig him up and throw stones at him. (George Bernard Shaw)

A new book says that Shakespeare was gay. In fact my boyfriend was the first guy to do him in the park. (David Corrado)

I was going to read a poem by Shakespeare the other day but then I thought: Why should I? He never read any of mine. (Spike Milligan)

William Wordsworth
Wordsworth wrote 'The prelude'
and that was all right.
But it was a prelude
to a lot of shite.
(Kingsley Amis)

William Wordsworth was very kind to me. He let me listen to him talking about himself. (Elizabeth Barrett Browning)

Women in Writing
Receptionist: How do you write women so well?
Melvin: I think of a man and I take away reason and accountability.
(Julie Benz and Jack Nicholson from *As Good As It Gets*)

Women Writers
The critics have started to call me a woman writer. Until they also speak of 'men writers', this is an insult. (Martha Gellhorn)

Words
I never write 'policeman' when I can get the same money for 'cop.' (Mark Twain)

Just because I don't use the ten dollar words doesn't mean I don't know them. (Ernest Hemingway)

Of every four words I write, I strike out three. (Niels Bohr)

If the word 'arse' is in a sentence, no matter how beautiful it is, the reader will react only to that. (Jules Renard)

Work Routines
First coffee, and after that a bowel movement. Then the muse assails me. (Gore Vidal)

Writer's Block
Lately my books are taking me as long as elephant's pregnancies. (Norman Mailer)

You could have built the Great Wall of China with the number of writer's blocks I've had. (Olaf Tyaransen)

Writer's block is a fancy term made up by whiners so they can have an excuse to drink alcohol. (Steve Martin)

Writers have two main problems. One is writer's block, when the words won't come, and the other is logorrhoea, when they come so fast you can hardly get them into the waste basket on time. (Cecilia Bartholomew)

Gazing at the typewriter in moments of desperation I console myself with three thoughts: Alcohol at six, dinner at eight, and to be immortal you've got to be dead. (Gyles Brandreth)

Writing
There's nothing wrong with writing as long as you do it in private and wash your hands afterwards. (Robert Heinlein)

I might have become a great writer but the chairs in the library were too hard. (Diane DiPrima)

X

X-Ratings
The words they put the Xs through are the ones that make you famous. (Norman Mailer)

Y

Young Writers
I'm often asked to give advice to young writers. I just tell them they're sick, that writing is an incurable illness. (Leonard Cohen)

Z

Zane Grey
If Grey went out with a mosquito net to catch minnows he could make it sound like a Roman gladiator setting forth to slay whales in the Tiber. (Robert Davies)